INVENTIONS AND DISCOVERY

PHILO FARNSWORTH and the TELEVISION

by Ellen Sturm Niz

illustrated by Keith Tucker

Consultant:

Raissa Allaire, Vice President/Chief of Staff
Museum of Broadcast Communications
Chicago, Illinois

Capstone
press®

Mankato, Minnesota

Graphic Library is published by Capstone Press,
151 Good Counsel Drive, P.O. Box 669, Mankato, Minnesota 56002.
www.capstonepub.com

Printed in the United States of America in Stevens Point, Wisconsin.
052011
006210R

 Books published by Capstone Press are manufactured with paper
containing at least 10 percent post-consumer waste.

Library of Congress Cataloging-in-Publication Data
Niz, Ellen Sturm.
    Philo Farnsworth and the television / by Ellen Sturm Niz; illustrated by Keith Tucker.
    p. cm.—(Graphic library. Inventions and discovery)
    Summary: "In graphic novel format, tells the story of how Philo Farnsworth came up with
the idea for electronic television at age 14, and later developed his idea into the technology for
television that is still used today"—Provided by publisher.
    Includes bibliographical references and index.
    ISBN-13: 978-0-7368-6487-9 (hardcover)
    ISBN-10: 0-7368-6487-3 (hardcover)
    ISBN-13: 978-0-7368-9649-8 (softcover pbk.)
    ISBN-10: 0-7368-9649-X (softcover pbk.)
    1. Farnsworth, Philo Taylor, 1906–1971—Juvenile literature. 2. Electric engineers—United
States—Biography—Juvenile literature. 3. Inventors—United States—Biography—Juvenile
literature. 4. Television—History—Juvenile literature. I. Tucker, Keith, ill. II. Title. III. Series.
TK6635.F3N59 2007
621.3880092–dc22
[B]   2006006395

Art Direction and Design
Jason Knudson and Juliette Peters

Colorist
Tami Collins

Editor
Christine Peterson

Editor's note: Direct quotations from primary sources are indicated by a yellow background.

Direct quotations appear on the following pages:
Page 15, from an interview with Elma Farnsworth as published in *The Boy Who Invented
    Television: A Story of Inspiration, Persistence, and Quiet Passion* by Paul Schatzkin (Silver
    Spring, Md.: TeamCom Books, 2002).
Page 21, from David Sarnoff's speech at the 1939 World's Fair as published in *Looking Ahead:
    The Papers of David Sarnoff* by David Sarnoff (New York: McGraw-Hill, 1968).
Page 25, quote attributed to Philo Farnsworth as published in *Distant Vision: Romance and
    Discovery on an Invisible Frontier* by Elma G. Farnsworth (Salt Lake City: PemberlyKent,
    1990).

TABLE OF CONTENTS

Chapter 1 The Boy Inventor

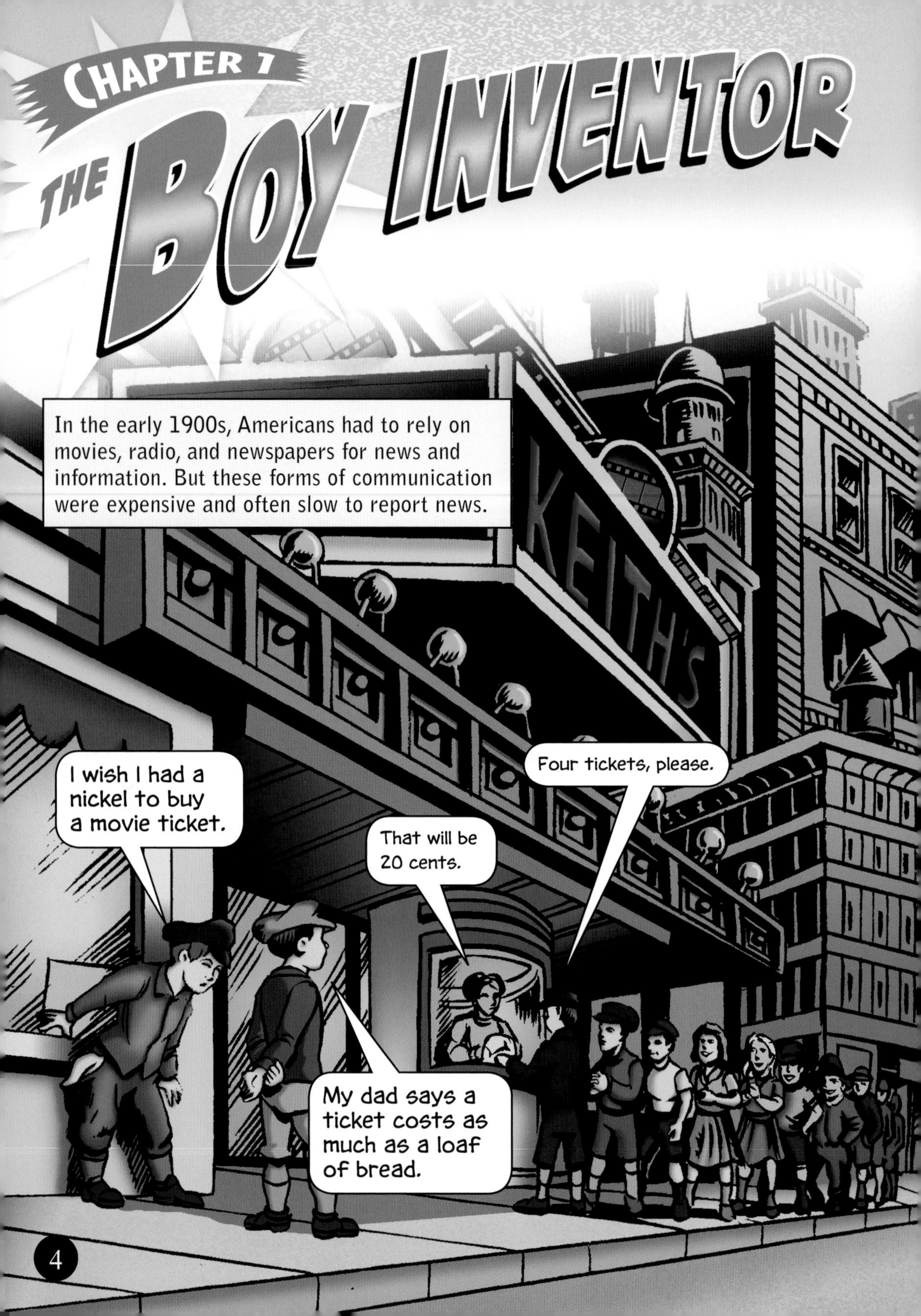
In the early 1900s, Americans had to rely on movies, radio, and newspapers for news and information. But these forms of communication were expensive and often slow to report news.
KEITH'S
I wish I had a nickel to buy a movie ticket.
My dad says a ticket costs as much as a loaf of bread.
Four tickets, please.
That will be 20 cents.

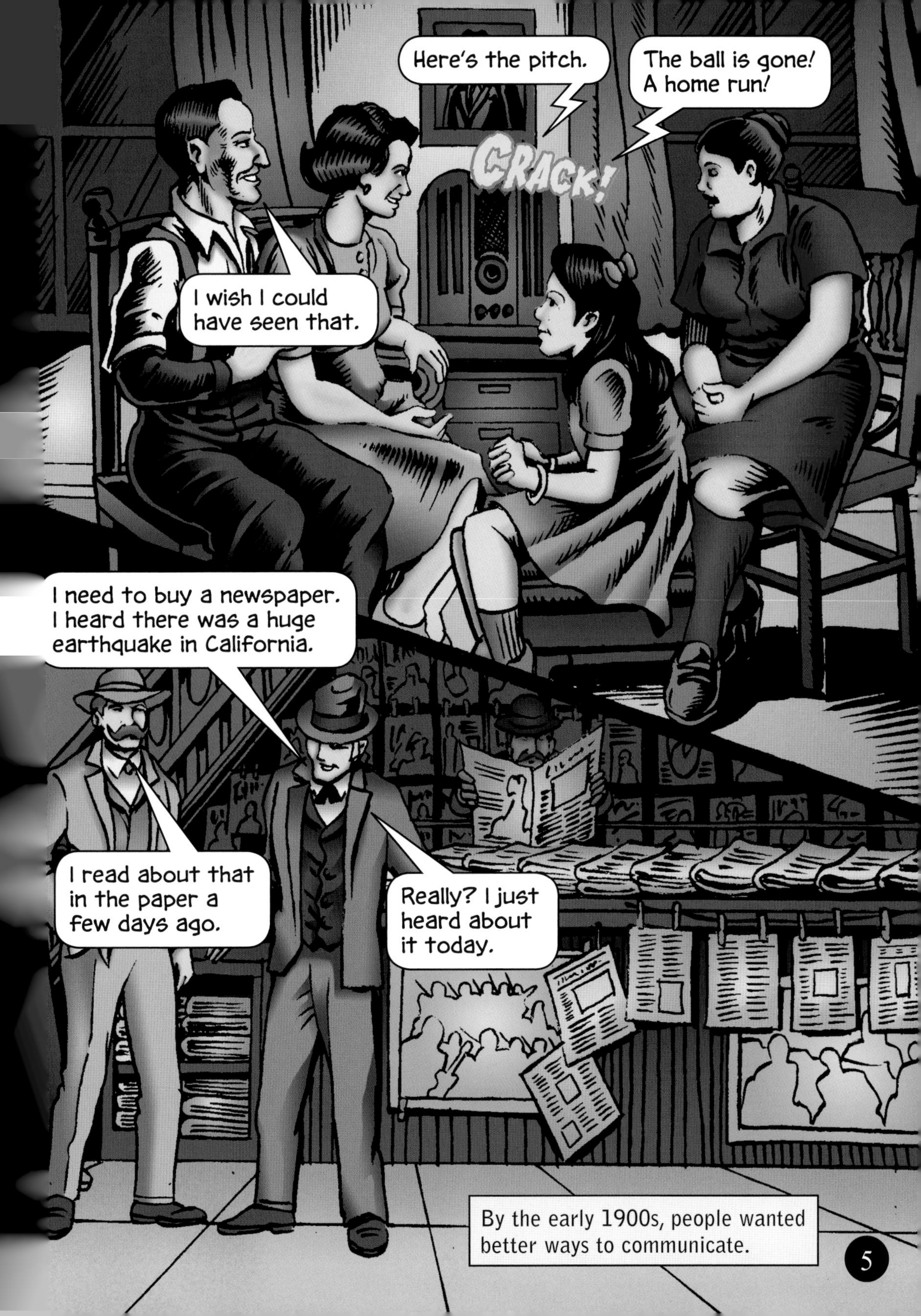
Here's the pitch.
CRACK!
The ball is gone! A home run!
I wish I could have seen that.
I need to buy a newspaper. I heard there was a huge earthquake in California.
I read about that in the paper a few days ago.
Really? I just heard about it today.

By the early 1900s, people wanted better ways to communicate.

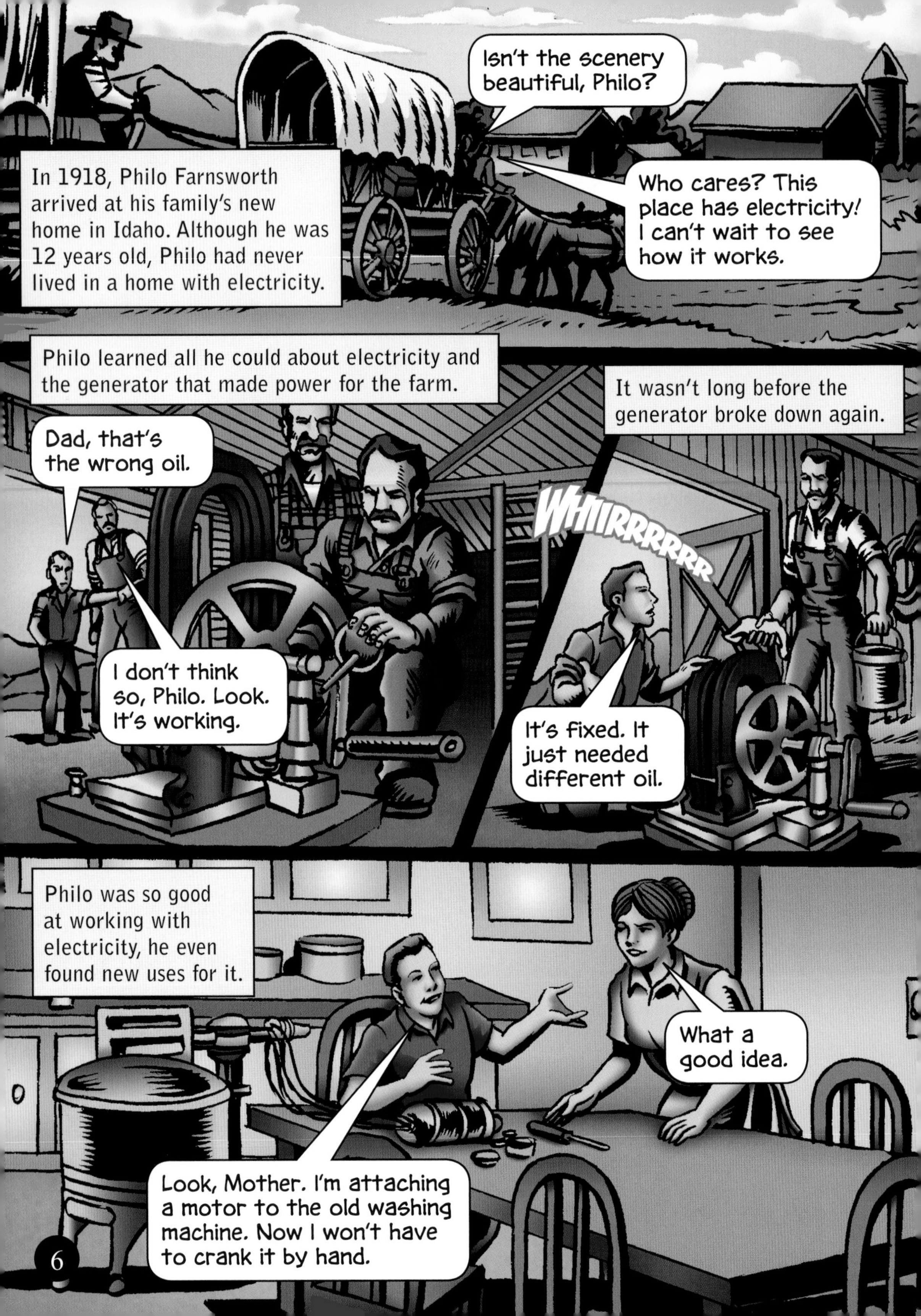
In 1918, Philo Farnsworth arrived at his family's new home in Idaho. Although he was 12 years old, Philo had never lived in a home with electricity.
Isn't the scenery beautiful, Philo?
Who cares? This place has electricity! I can't wait to see how it works.
Philo learned all he could about electricity and the generator that made power for the farm.
Dad, that's the wrong oil.
I don't think so, Philo. Look. It's working.
It wasn't long before the generator broke down again.
WHIIRRRRRRR
It's fixed. It just needed different oil.
Philo was so good at working with electricity, he even found new uses for it.
What a good idea.
Look, Mother. I'm attaching a motor to the old washing machine. Now I won't have to crank it by hand.

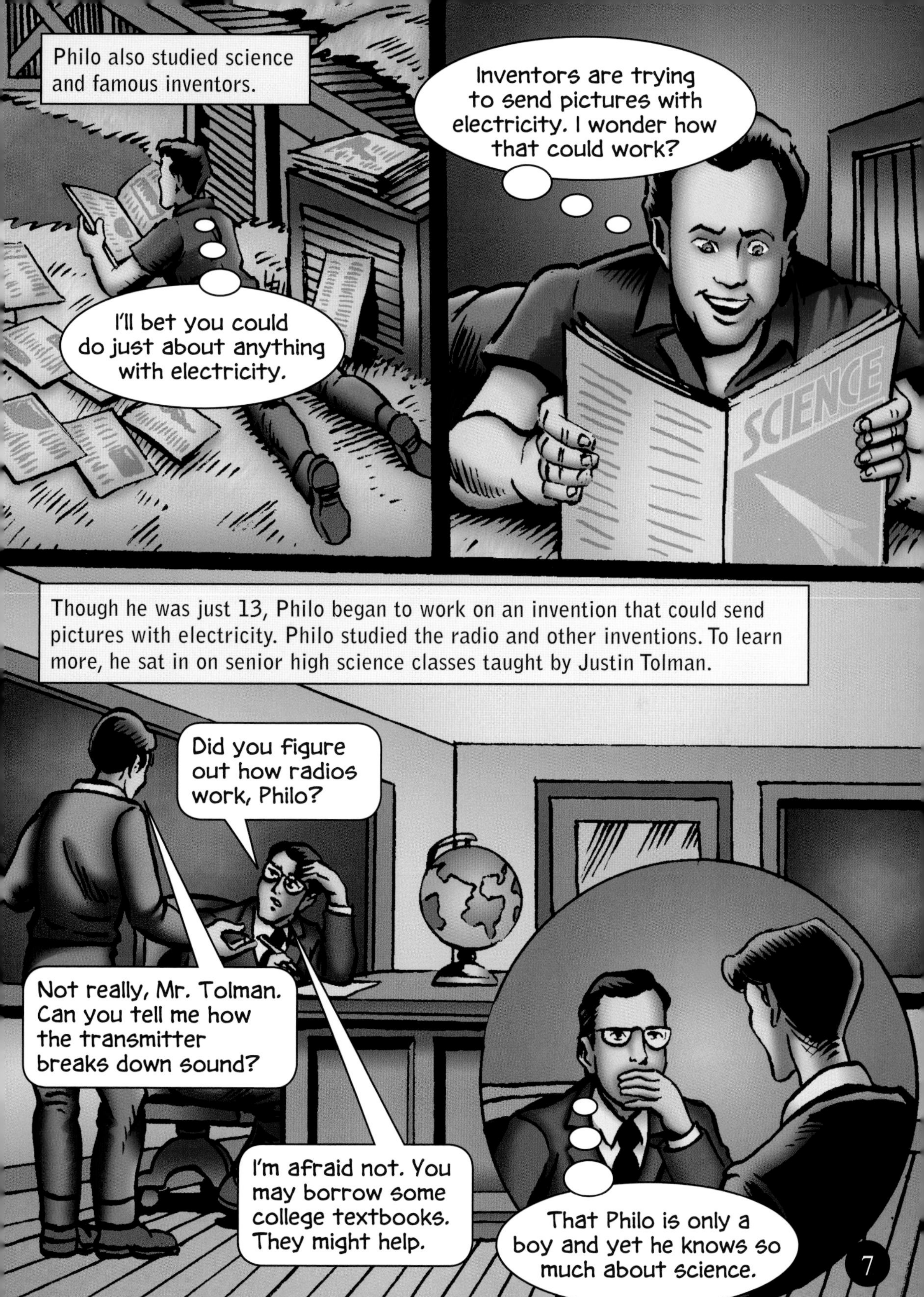
Philo also studied science and famous inventors.
I'll bet you could do just about anything with electricity.
Inventors are trying to send pictures with electricity. I wonder how that could work?
SCIENCE
Though he was just 13, Philo began to work on an invention that could send pictures with electricity. Philo studied the radio and other inventions. To learn more, he sat in on senior high science classes taught by Justin Tolman.
Did you figure out how radios work, Philo?
Not really, Mr. Tolman. Can you tell me how the transmitter breaks down sound?
I'm afraid not. You may borrow some college textbooks. They might help.
That Philo is only a boy and yet he knows so much about science.

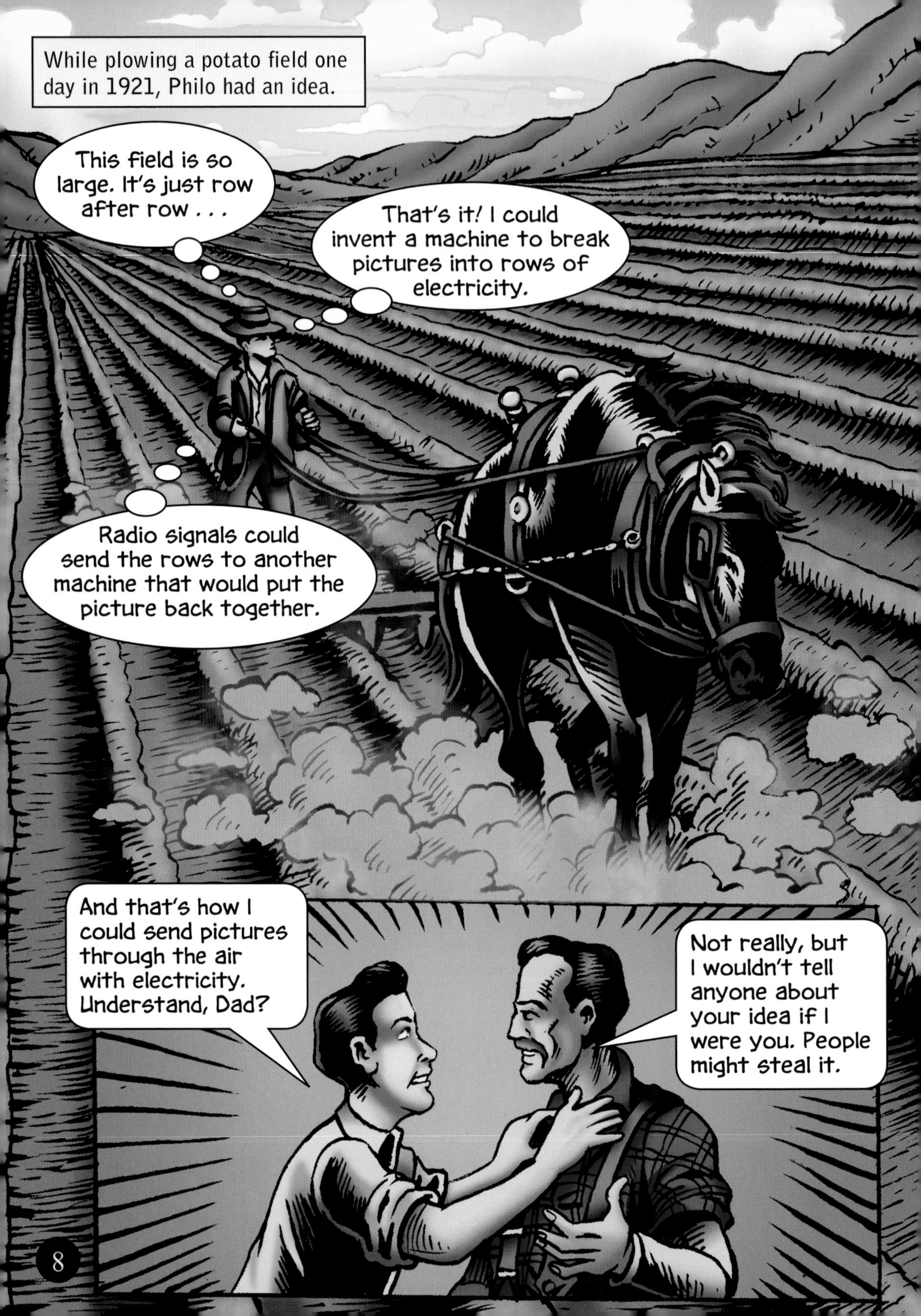
While plowing a potato field one day in 1921, Philo had an idea.
This field is so large. It's just row after row . . .
That's it! I could invent a machine to break pictures into rows of electricity.
Radio signals could send the rows to another machine that would put the picture back together.
And that's how I could send pictures through the air with electricity. Understand, Dad?
Not really, but I wouldn't tell anyone about your idea if I were you. People might steal it.

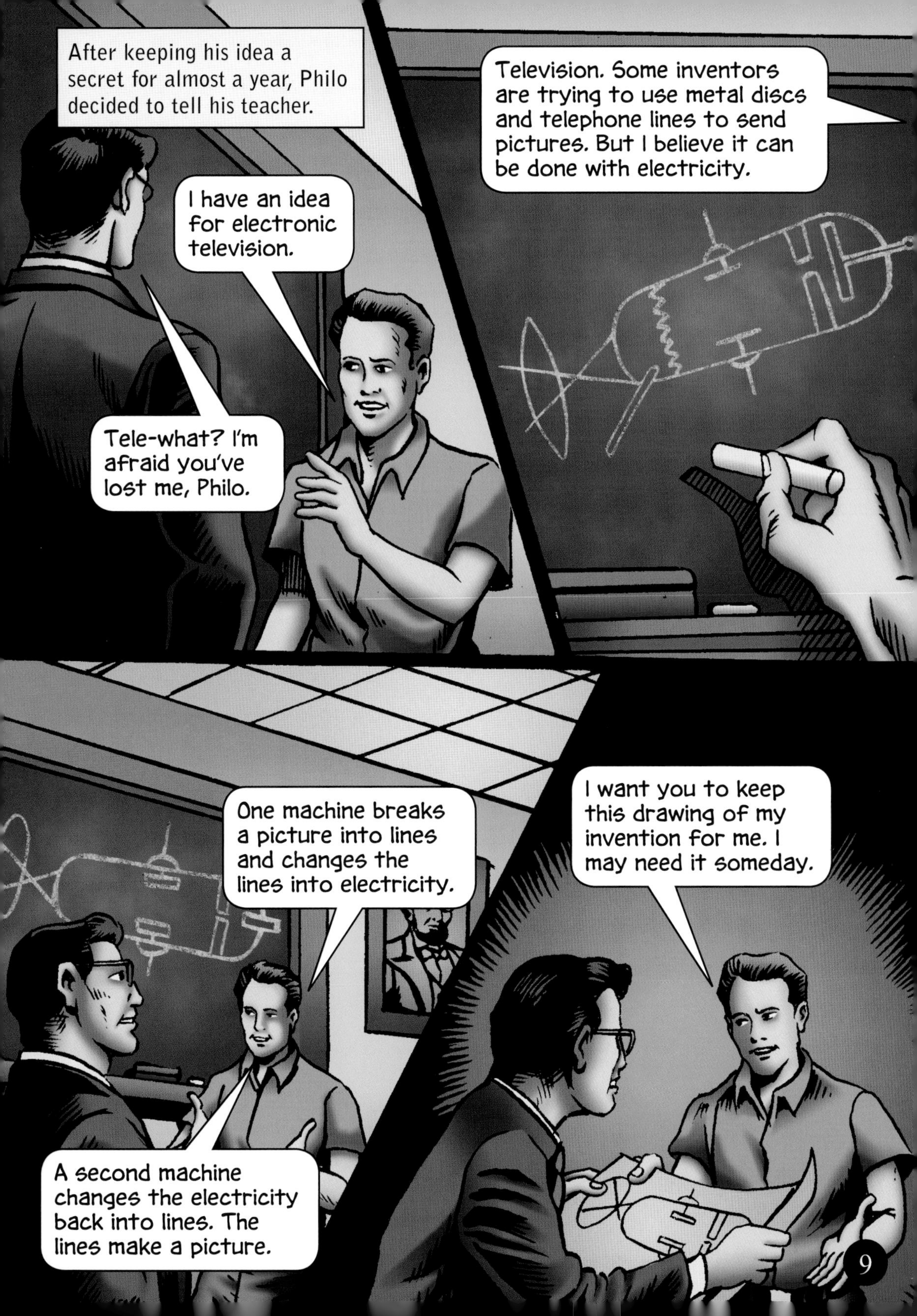
After keeping his idea a secret for almost a year, Philo decided to tell his teacher.
I have an idea for electronic television.
Tele-what? I'm afraid you've lost me, Philo.
Television. Some inventors are trying to use metal discs and telephone lines to send pictures. But I believe it can be done with electricity.
One machine breaks a picture into lines and changes the lines into electricity.
A second machine changes the electricity back into lines. The lines make a picture.
I want you to keep this drawing of my invention for me. I may need it someday.

Chapter 2
Building a Dream

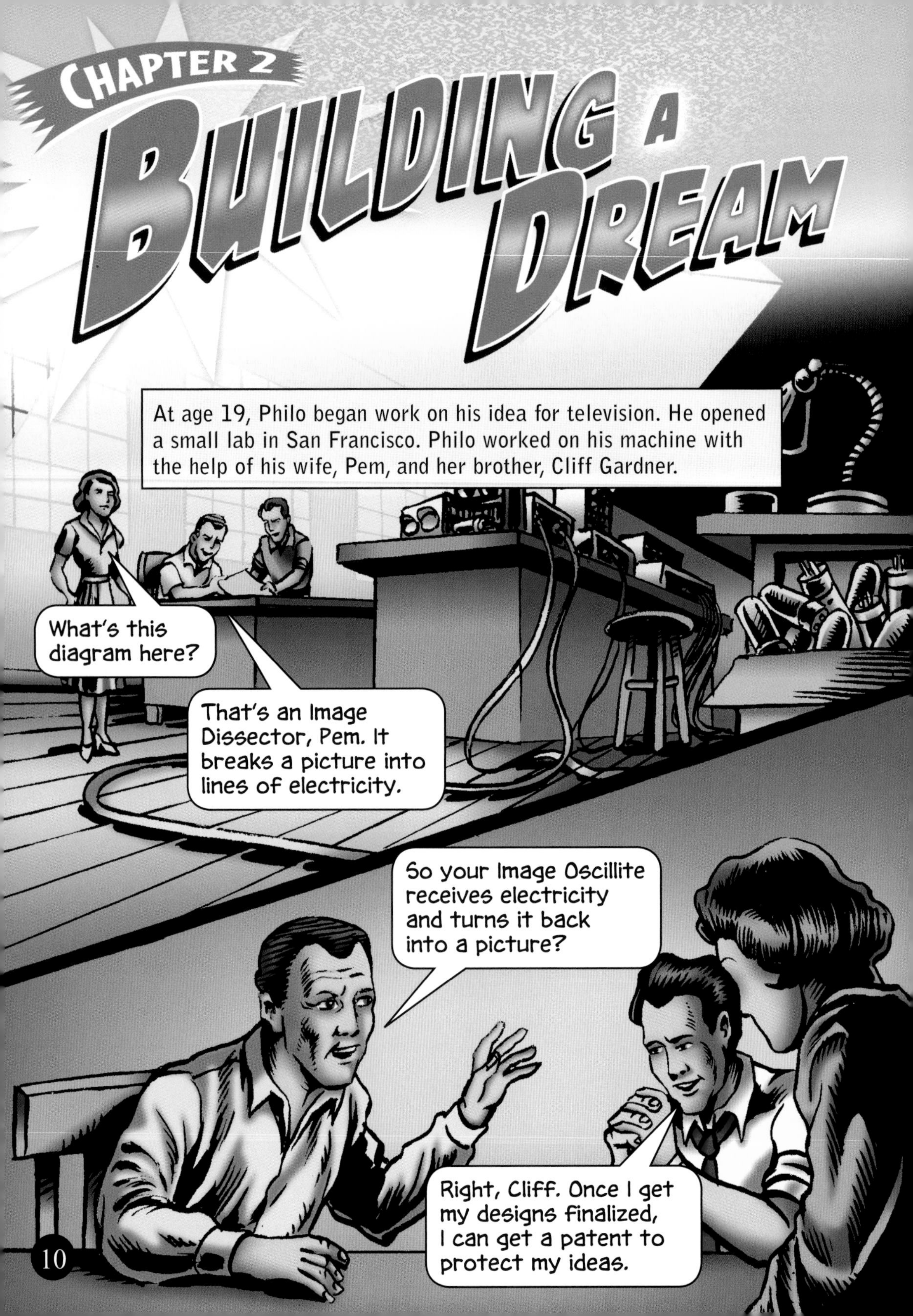
At age 19, Philo began work on his idea for television. He opened a small lab in San Francisco. Philo worked on his machine with the help of his wife, Pem, and her brother, Cliff Gardner.
What's this diagram here?
That's an Image Dissector, Pem. It breaks a picture into lines of electricity.
So your Image Oscillite receives electricity and turns it back into a picture?
Right, Cliff. Once I get my designs finalized, I can get a patent to protect my ideas.

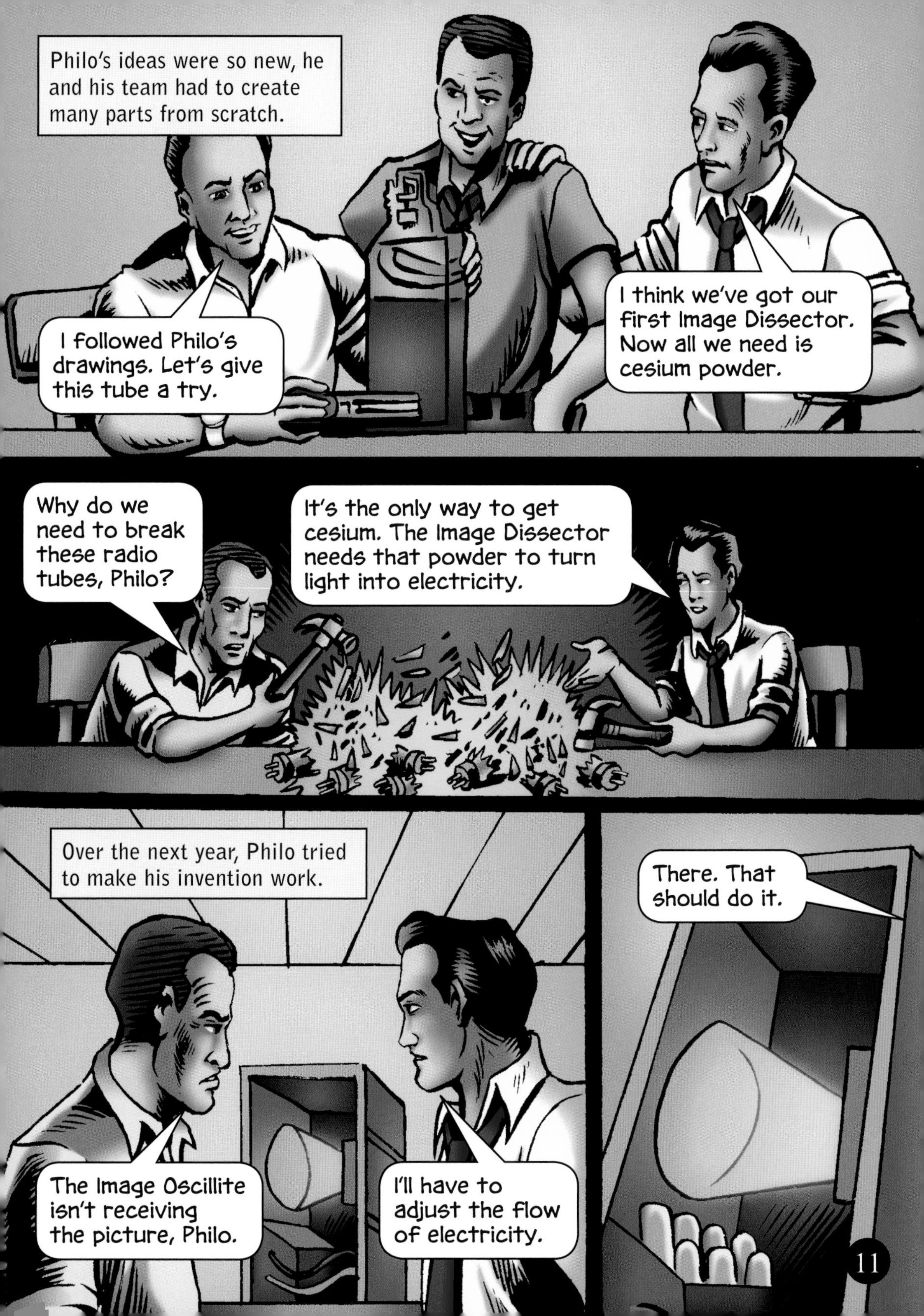

Philo's ideas were so new, he and his team had to create many parts from scratch.
I followed Philo's drawings. Let's give this tube a try.
I think we've got our first Image Dissector. Now all we need is cesium powder.
Why do we need to break these radio tubes, Philo?
It's the only way to get cesium. The Image Dissector needs that powder to turn light into electricity.
Over the next year, Philo tried to make his invention work.
The Image Oscillite isn't receiving the picture, Philo.
I'll have to adjust the flow of electricity.
There. That should do it.

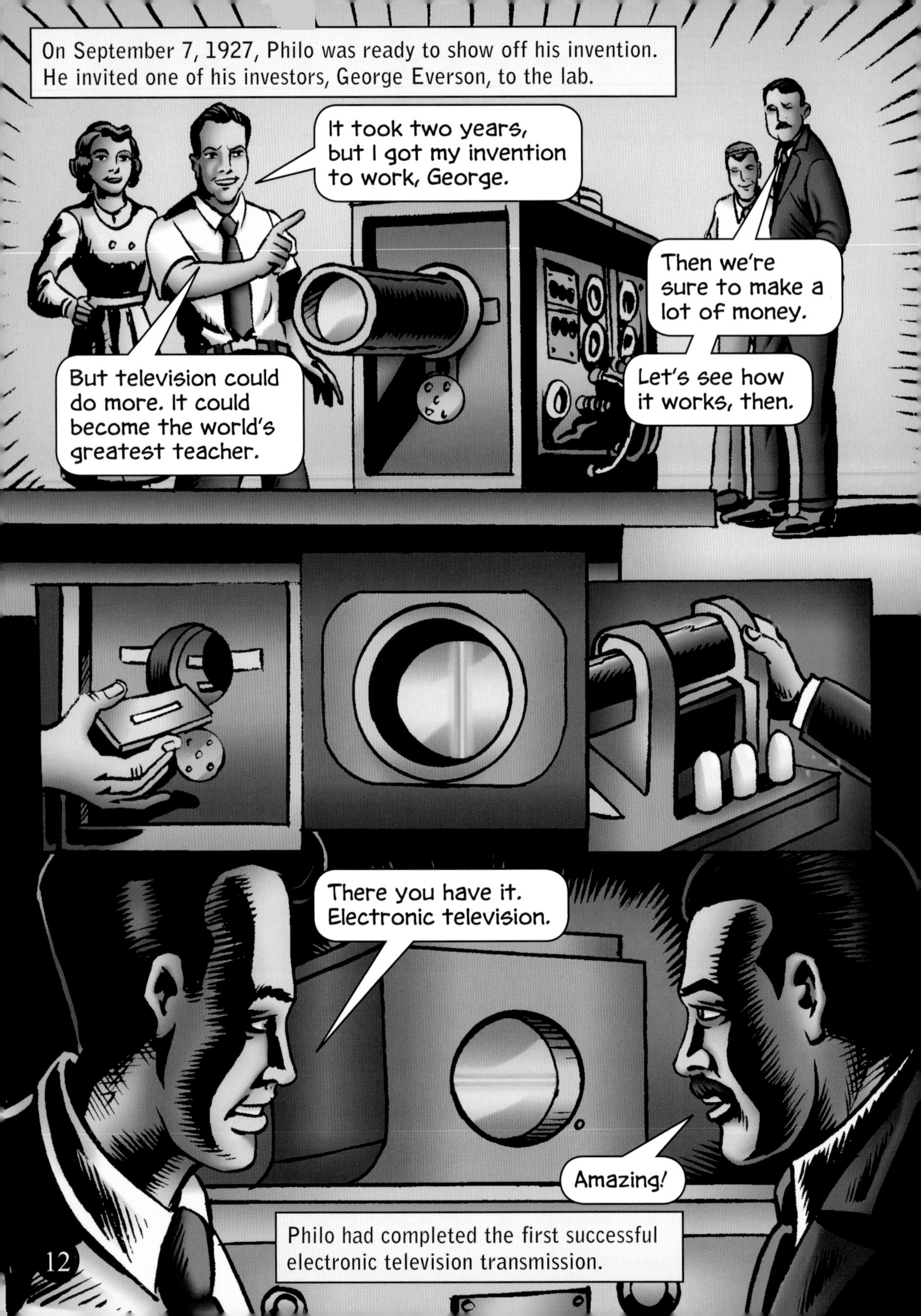
On September 7, 1927, Philo was ready to show off his invention. He invited one of his investors, George Everson, to the lab.
It took two years, but I got my invention to work, George.
Then we're sure to make a lot of money.
But television could do more. It could become the world's greatest teacher.
Let's see how it works, then.
There you have it. Electronic television.
Amazing!
Philo had completed the first successful electronic television transmission.

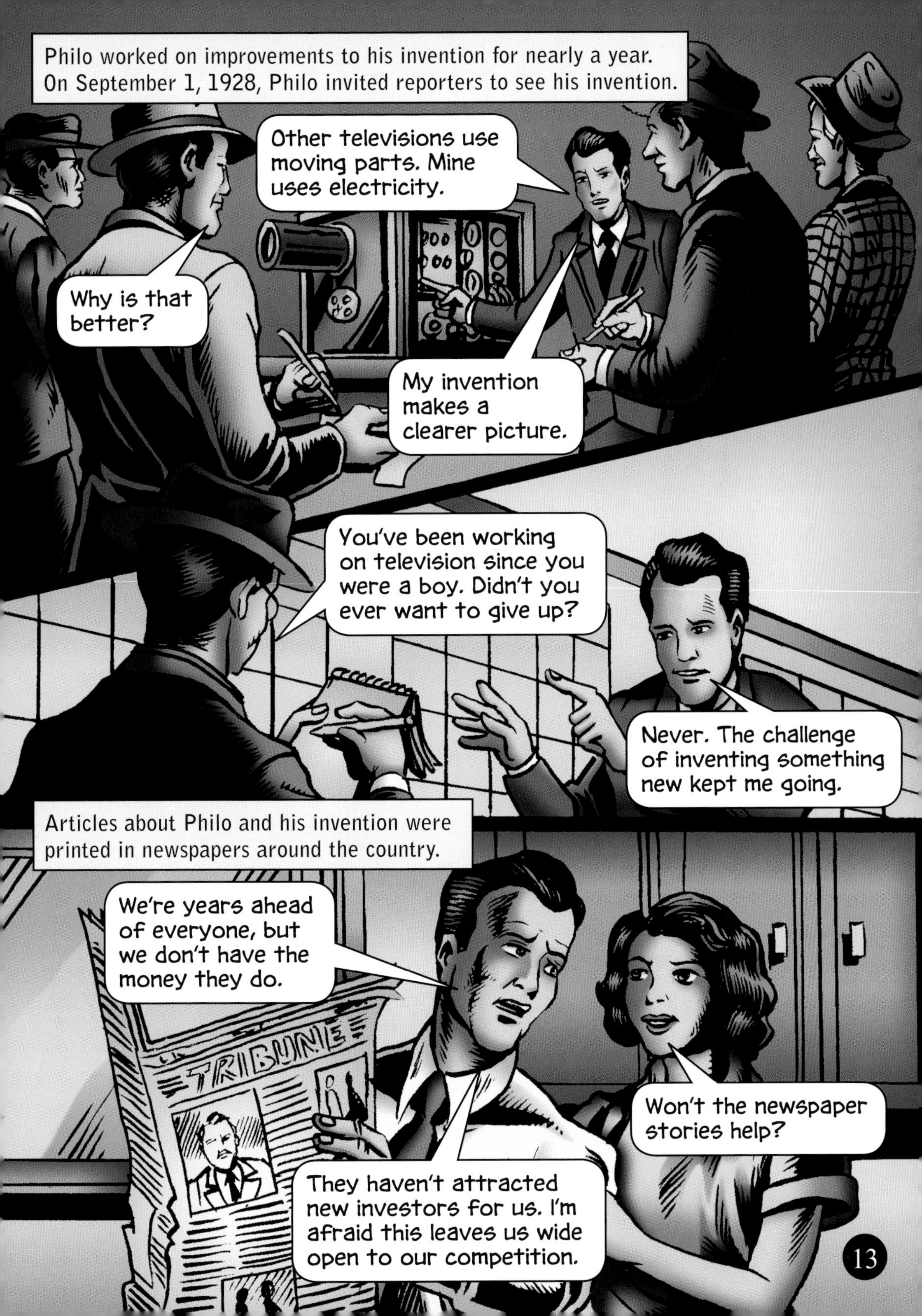
Philo worked on improvements to his invention for nearly a year. On September 1, 1928, Philo invited reporters to see his invention.
Other televisions use moving parts. Mine uses electricity.
Why is that better?
My invention makes a clearer picture.
You've been working on television since you were a boy. Didn't you ever want to give up?
Never. The challenge of inventing something new kept me going.
Articles about Philo and his invention were printed in newspapers around the country.
We're years ahead of everyone, but we don't have the money they do.
TRIBUNE
Won't the newspaper stories help?
They haven't attracted new investors for us. I'm afraid this leaves us wide open to our competition.

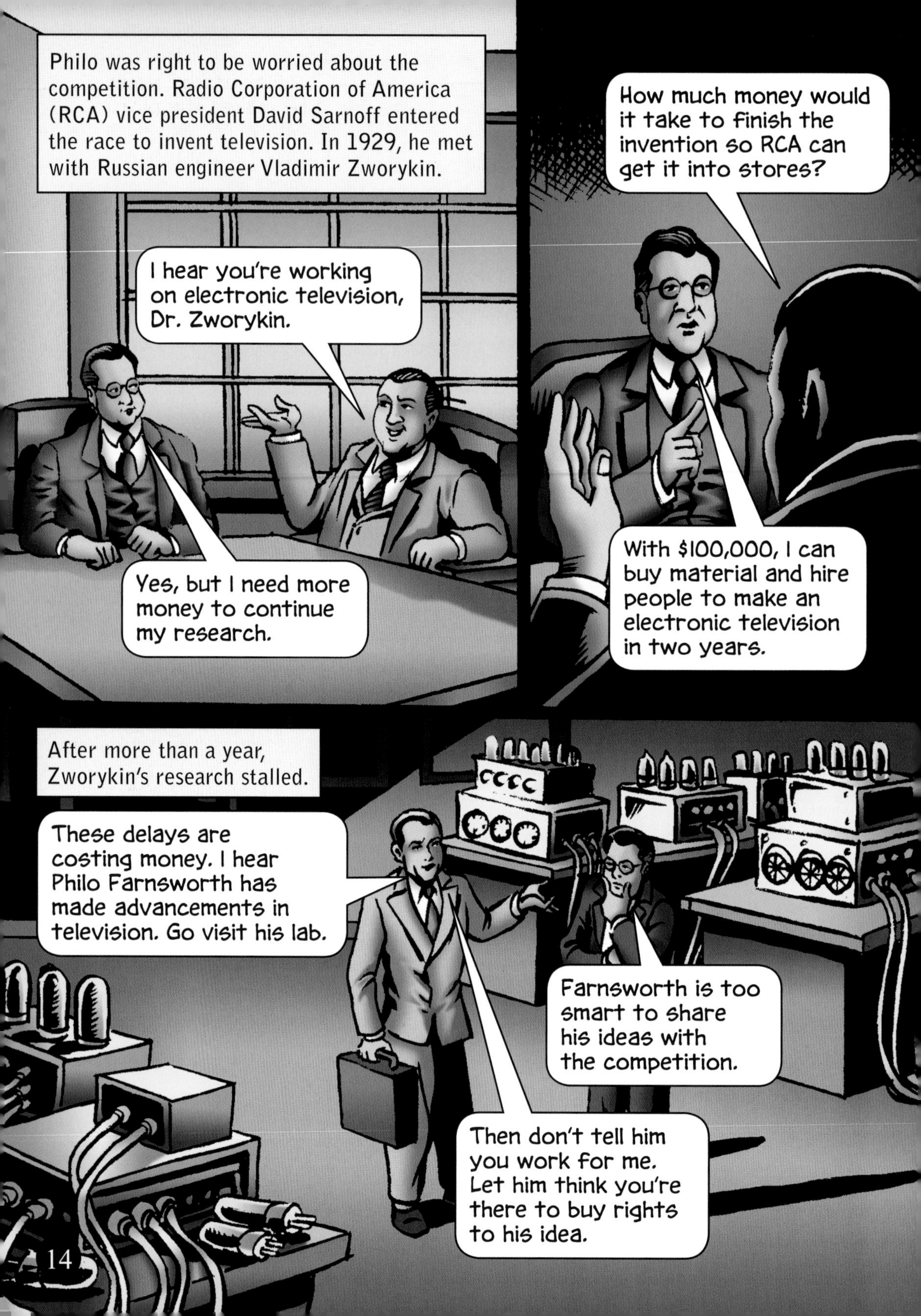

Philo was right to be worried about the competition. Radio Corporation of America (RCA) vice president David Sarnoff entered the race to invent television. In 1929, he met with Russian engineer Vladimir Zworykin.
I hear you're working on electronic television, Dr. Zworykin.
Yes, but I need more money to continue my research.
How much money would it take to finish the invention so RCA can get it into stores?
With $100,000, I can buy material and hire people to make an electronic television in two years.
After more than a year, Zworykin's research stalled.
These delays are costing money. I hear Philo Farnsworth has made advancements in television. Go visit his lab.
Farnsworth is too smart to share his ideas with the competition.
Then don't tell him you work for me. Let him think you're there to buy rights to his idea.

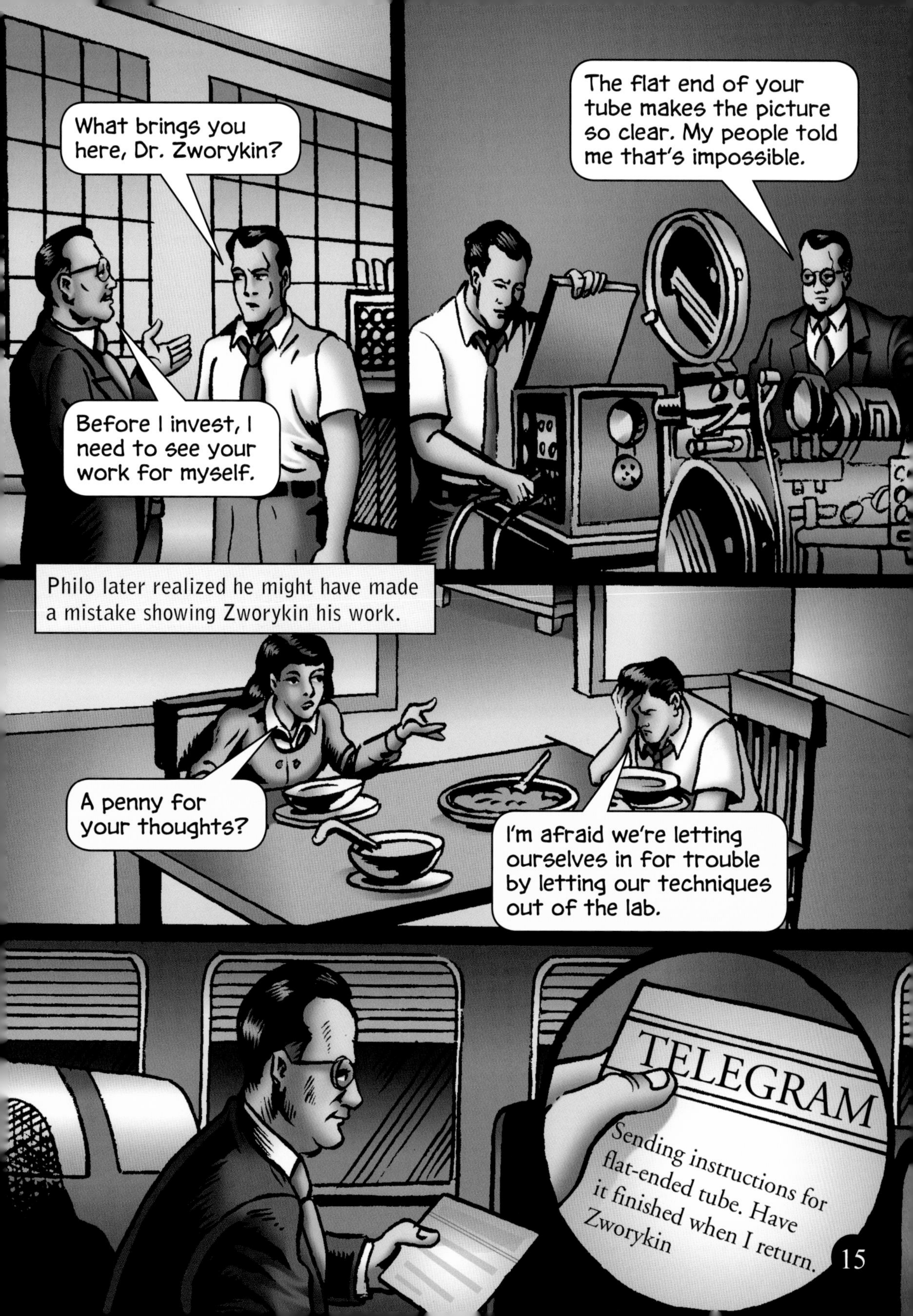
What brings you here, Dr. Zworykin?
Before I invest, I need to see your work for myself.
The flat end of your tube makes the picture so clear. My people told me that's impossible.
Philo later realized he might have made a mistake showing Zworykin his work.
A penny for your thoughts?
I'm afraid we're letting ourselves in for trouble by letting our techniques out of the lab.
TELEGRAM
Sending instructions for flat-ended tube. Have it finished when I return.
Zworykin

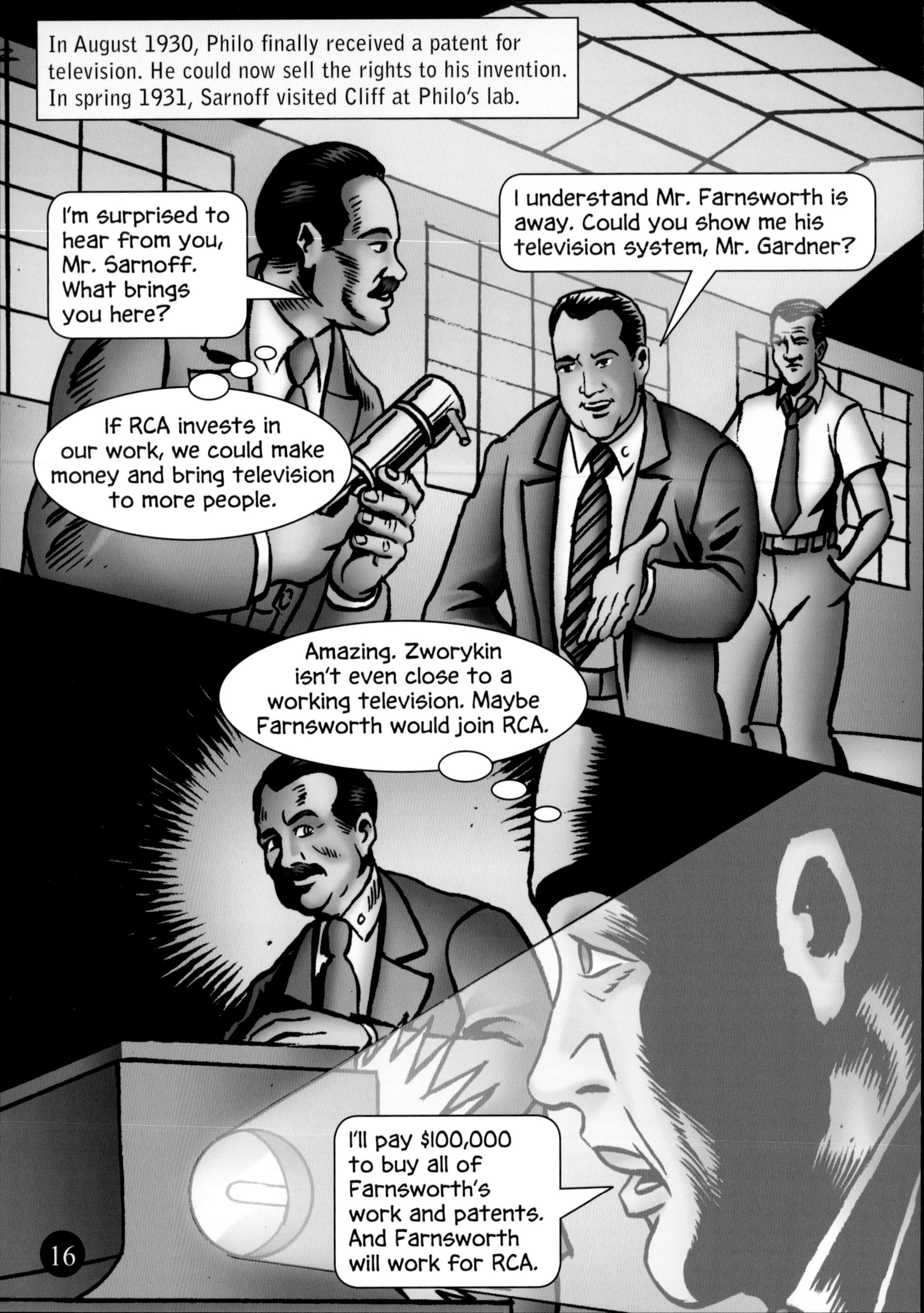
In August 1930, Philo finally received a patent for television. He could now sell the rights to his invention. In spring 1931, Sarnoff visited Cliff at Philo's lab.
I'm surprised to hear from you, Mr. Sarnoff. What brings you here?
I understand Mr. Farnsworth is away. Could you show me his television system, Mr. Gardner?
If RCA invests in our work, we could make money and bring television to more people.
Amazing. Zworykin isn't even close to a working television. Maybe Farnsworth would join RCA.
I'll pay $100,000 to buy all of Farnsworth's work and patents. And Farnsworth will work for RCA.

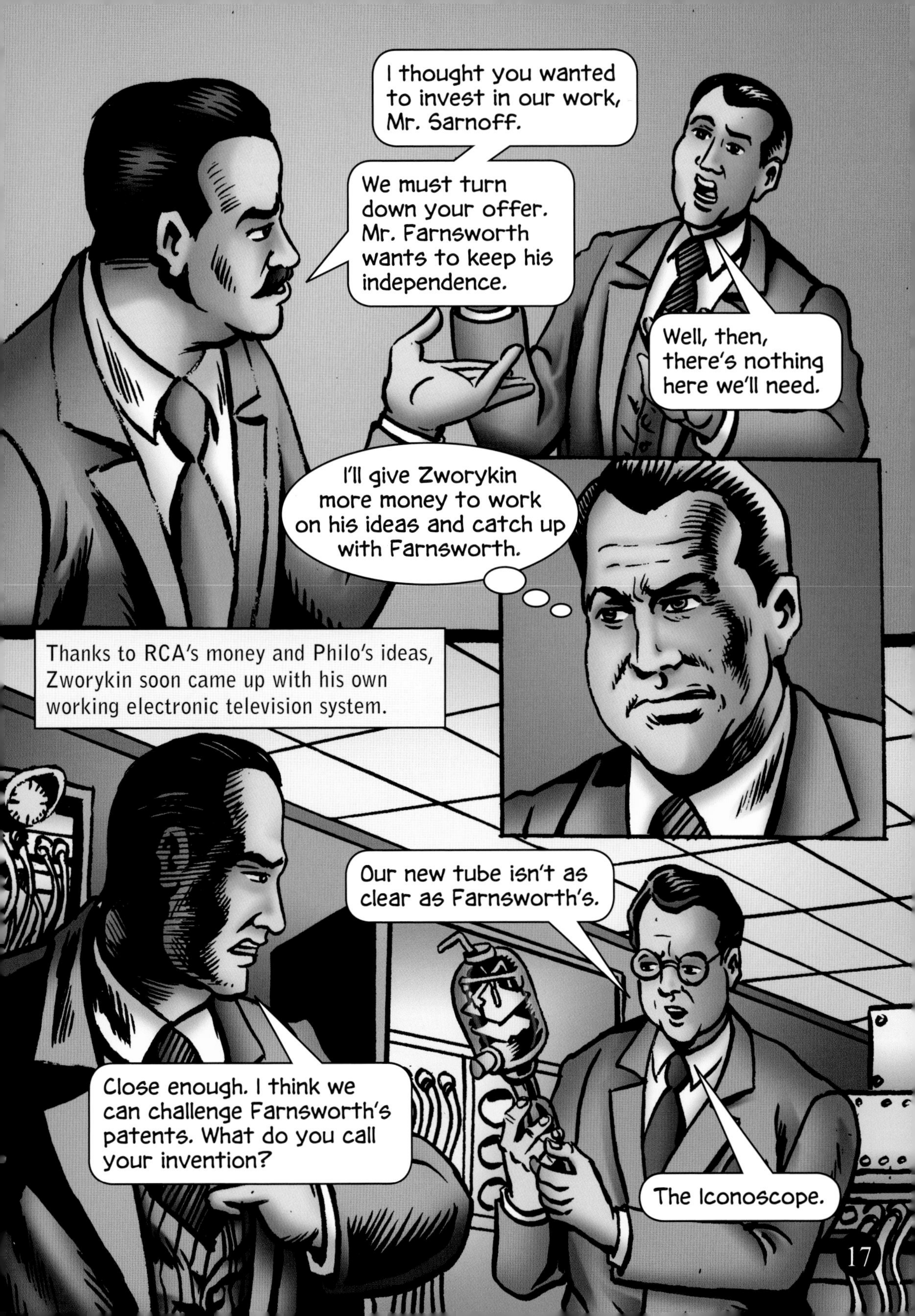
I thought you wanted to invest in our work, Mr. Sarnoff.
We must turn down your offer. Mr. Farnsworth wants to keep his independence.
Well, then, there's nothing here we'll need.
I'll give Zworykin more money to work on his ideas and catch up with Farnsworth.
Thanks to RCA's money and Philo's ideas, Zworykin soon came up with his own working electronic television system.
Our new tube isn't as clear as Farnsworth's.
Close enough. I think we can challenge Farnsworth's patents. What do you call your invention?
The Iconoscope.

Chapter 3
Television Takes Off

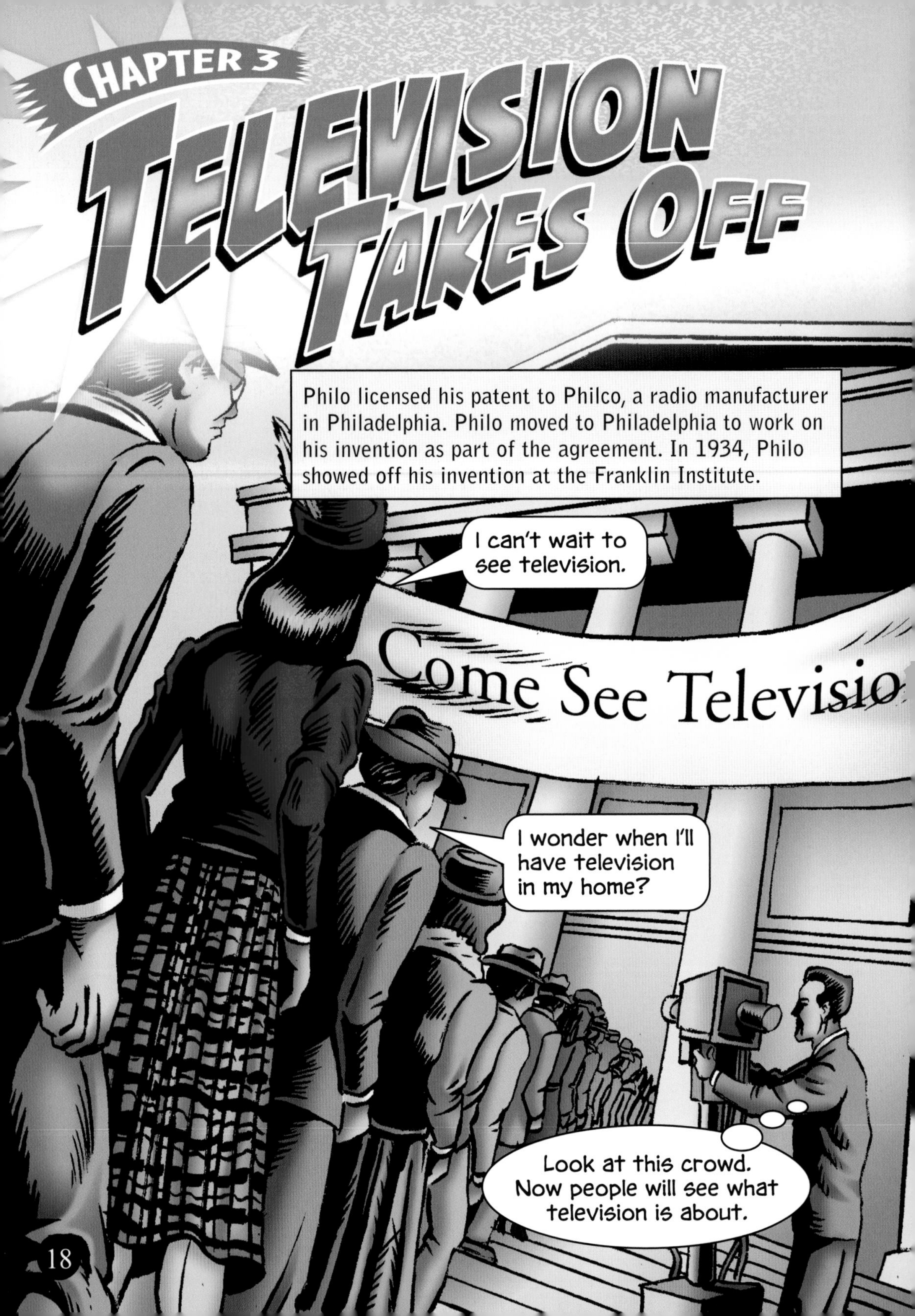
Philo licensed his patent to Philco, a radio manufacturer in Philadelphia. Philo moved to Philadelphia to work on his invention as part of the agreement. In 1934, Philo showed off his invention at the Franklin Institute.
I can't wait to see television.
Come See Televisio
I wonder when I'll have television in my home?
Look at this crowd. Now people will see what television is about.

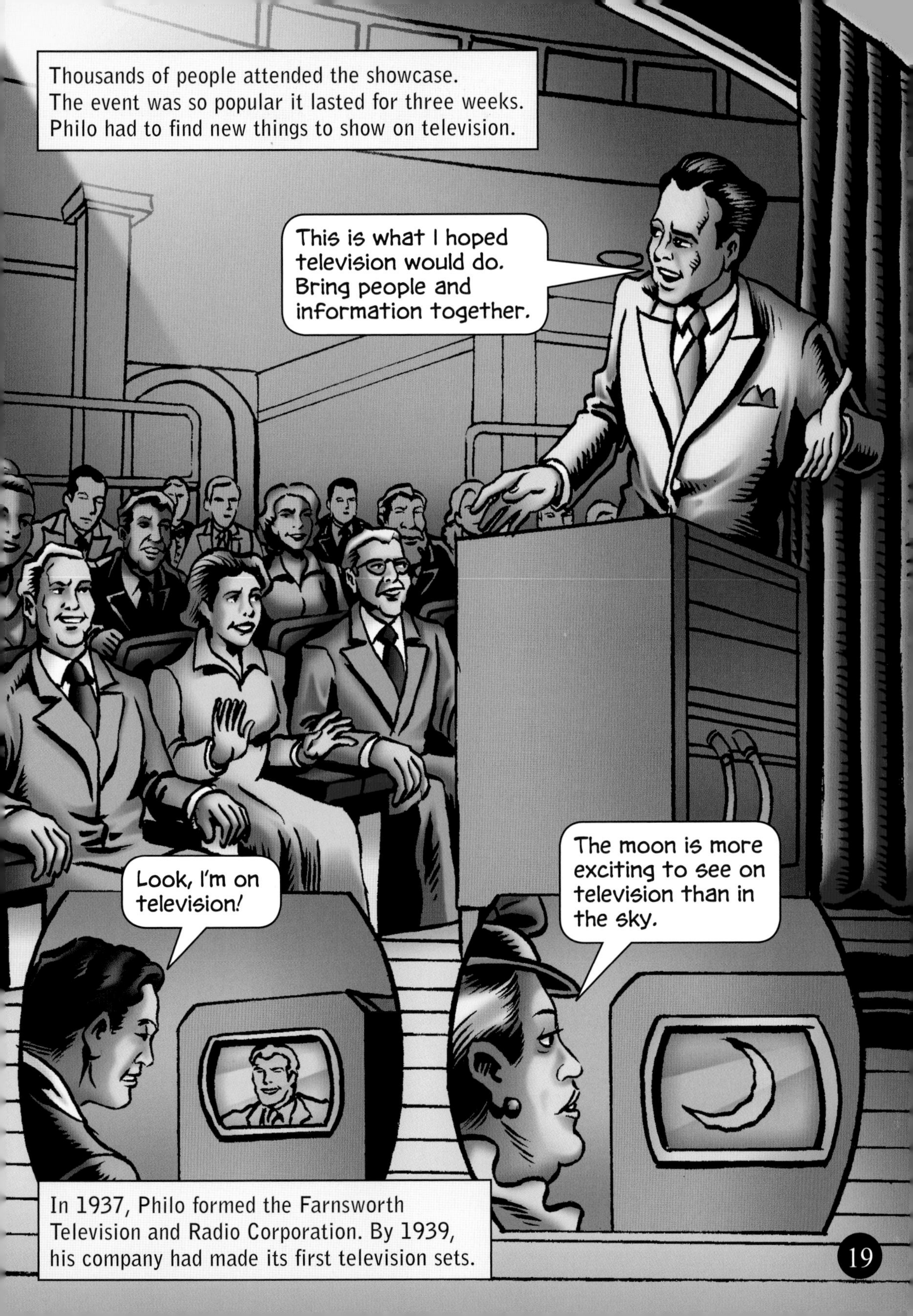

Thousands of people attended the showcase. The event was so popular it lasted for three weeks. Philo had to find new things to show on television.
This is what I hoped television would do. Bring people and information together.
Look, I'm on television!
The moon is more exciting to see on television than in the sky.
In 1937, Philo formed the Farnsworth Television and Radio Corporation. By 1939, his company had made its first television sets.

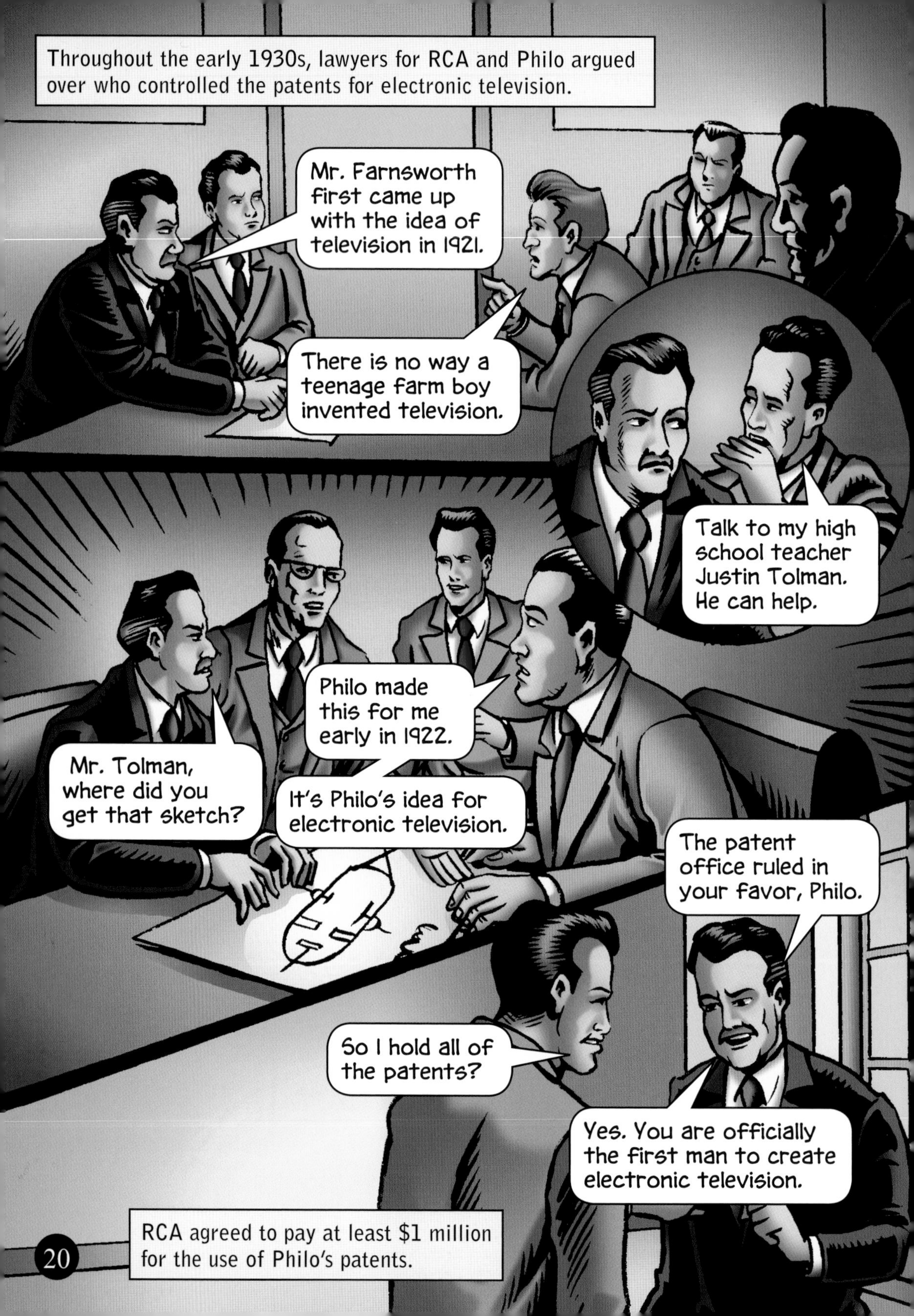
Throughout the early 1930s, lawyers for RCA and Philo argued over who controlled the patents for electronic television.
Mr. Farnsworth first came up with the idea of television in 1921.
There is no way a teenage farm boy invented television.
Talk to my high school teacher Justin Tolman. He can help.
Mr. Tolman, where did you get that sketch?
Philo made this for me early in 1922.
It's Philo's idea for electronic television.
The patent office ruled in your favor, Philo.
So I hold all of the patents?
Yes. You are officially the first man to create electronic television.
RCA agreed to pay at least $1 million for the use of Philo's patents.

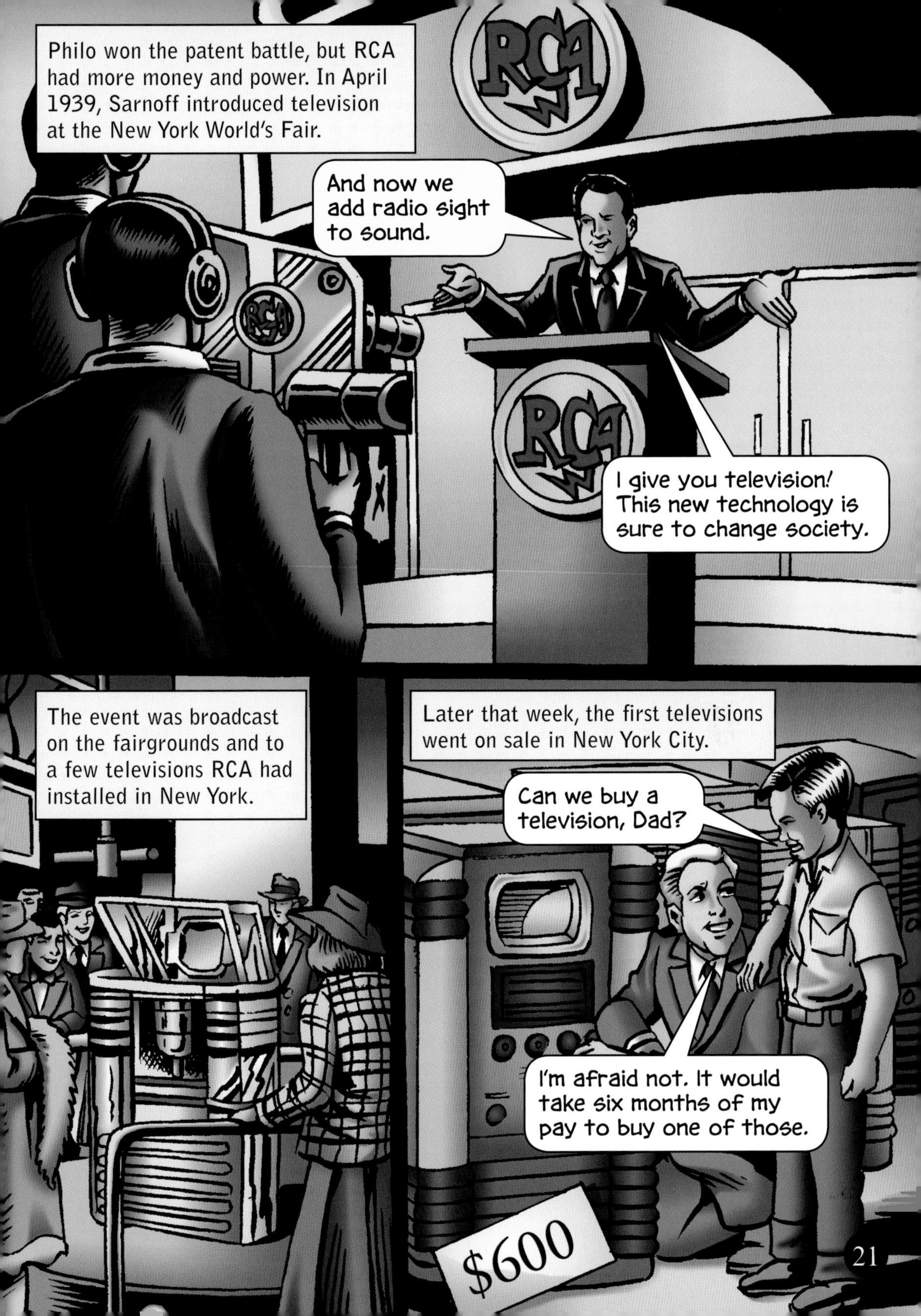
Philo won the patent battle, but RCA had more money and power. In April 1939, Sarnoff introduced television at the New York World's Fair.
And now we add radio sight to sound.
I give you television! This new technology is sure to change society.
The event was broadcast on the fairgrounds and to a few televisions RCA had installed in New York.
Later that week, the first televisions went on sale in New York City.
Can we buy a television, Dad?
I'm afraid not. It would take six months of my pay to buy one of those.
$600

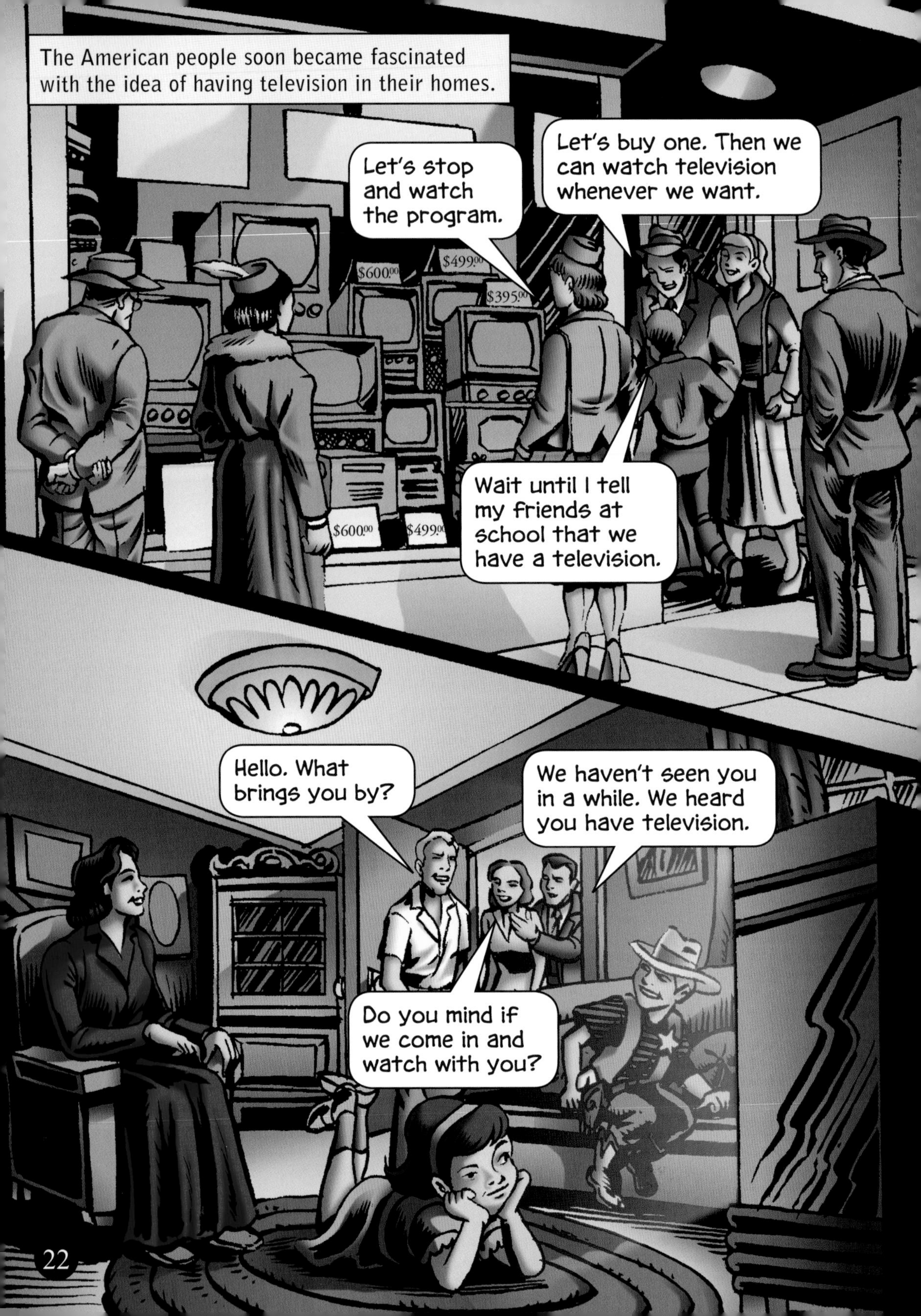
The American people soon became fascinated with the idea of having television in their homes.
$600.00
$499.00
$395.00
Let's stop and watch the program.
Let's buy one. Then we can watch television whenever we want.
Wait until I tell my friends at school that we have a television.
$600.00
$499.00
Hello. What brings you by?
We haven't seen you in a while. We heard you have television.
Do you mind if we come in and watch with you?

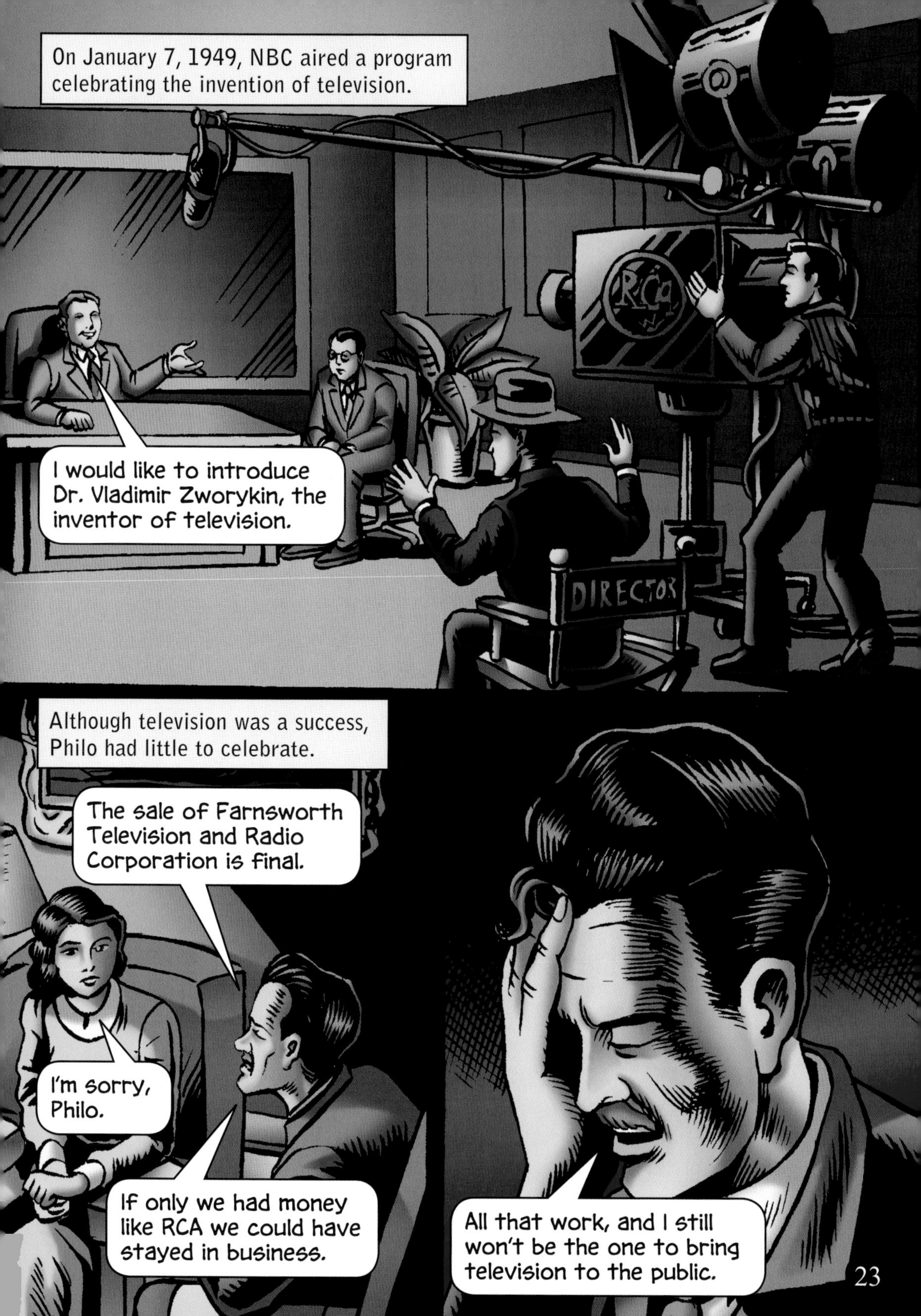
On January 7, 1949, NBC aired a program celebrating the invention of television.
I would like to introduce Dr. Vladimir Zworykin, the inventor of television.
RCA
DIRECTOR
Although television was a success, Philo had little to celebrate.
The sale of Farnsworth Television and Radio Corporation is final.
I'm sorry, Philo.
If only we had money like RCA we could have stayed in business.
All that work, and I still won't be the one to bring television to the public.

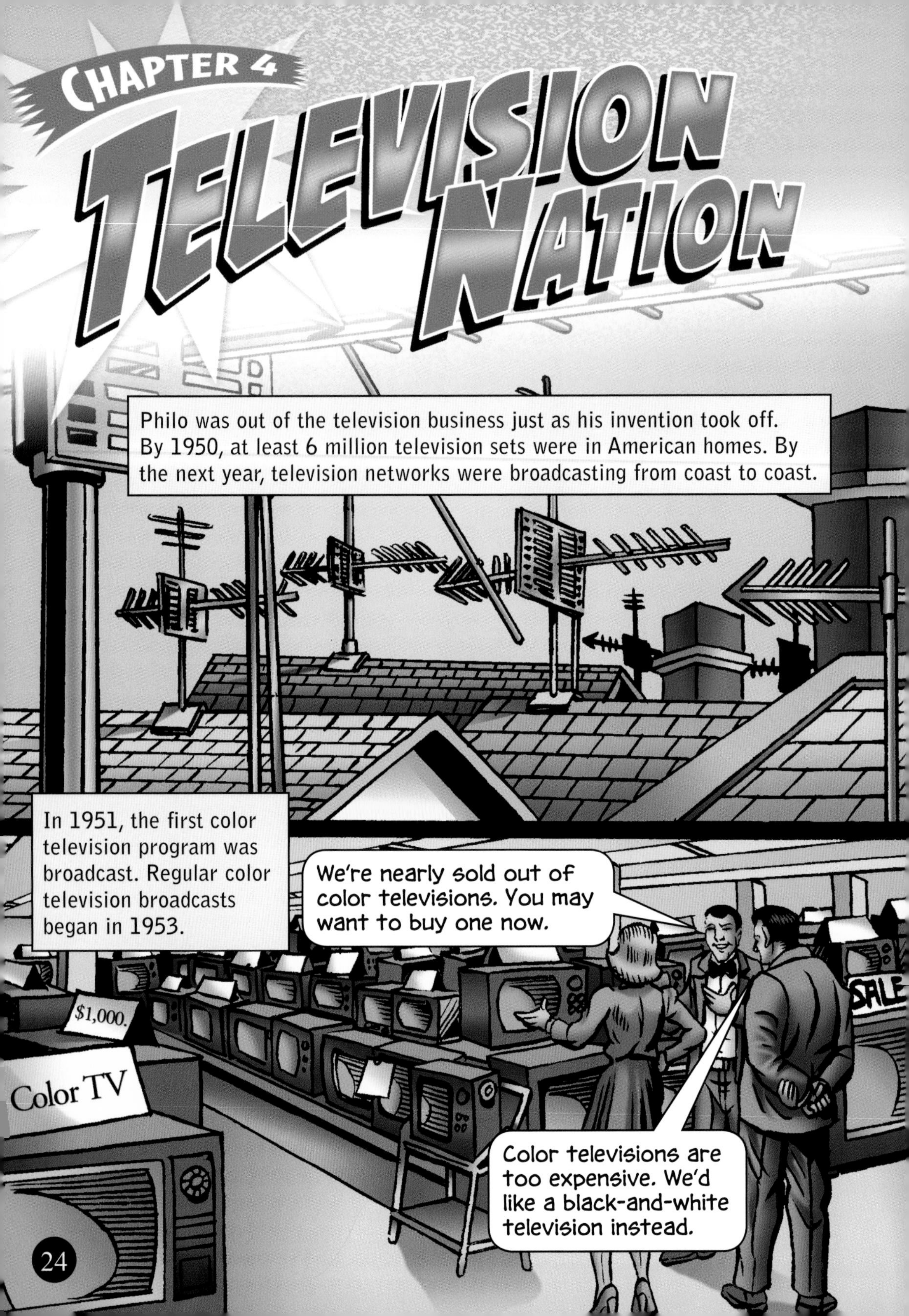
CHAPTER 4
TELEVISION NATION
Philo was out of the television business just as his invention took off. By 1950, at least 6 million television sets were in American homes. By the next year, television networks were broadcasting from coast to coast.
In 1951, the first color television program was broadcast. Regular color television broadcasts began in 1953.
We're nearly sold out of color televisions. You may want to buy one now.
$1,000.
Color TV
SALE
Color televisions are too expensive. We'd like a black-and-white television instead.

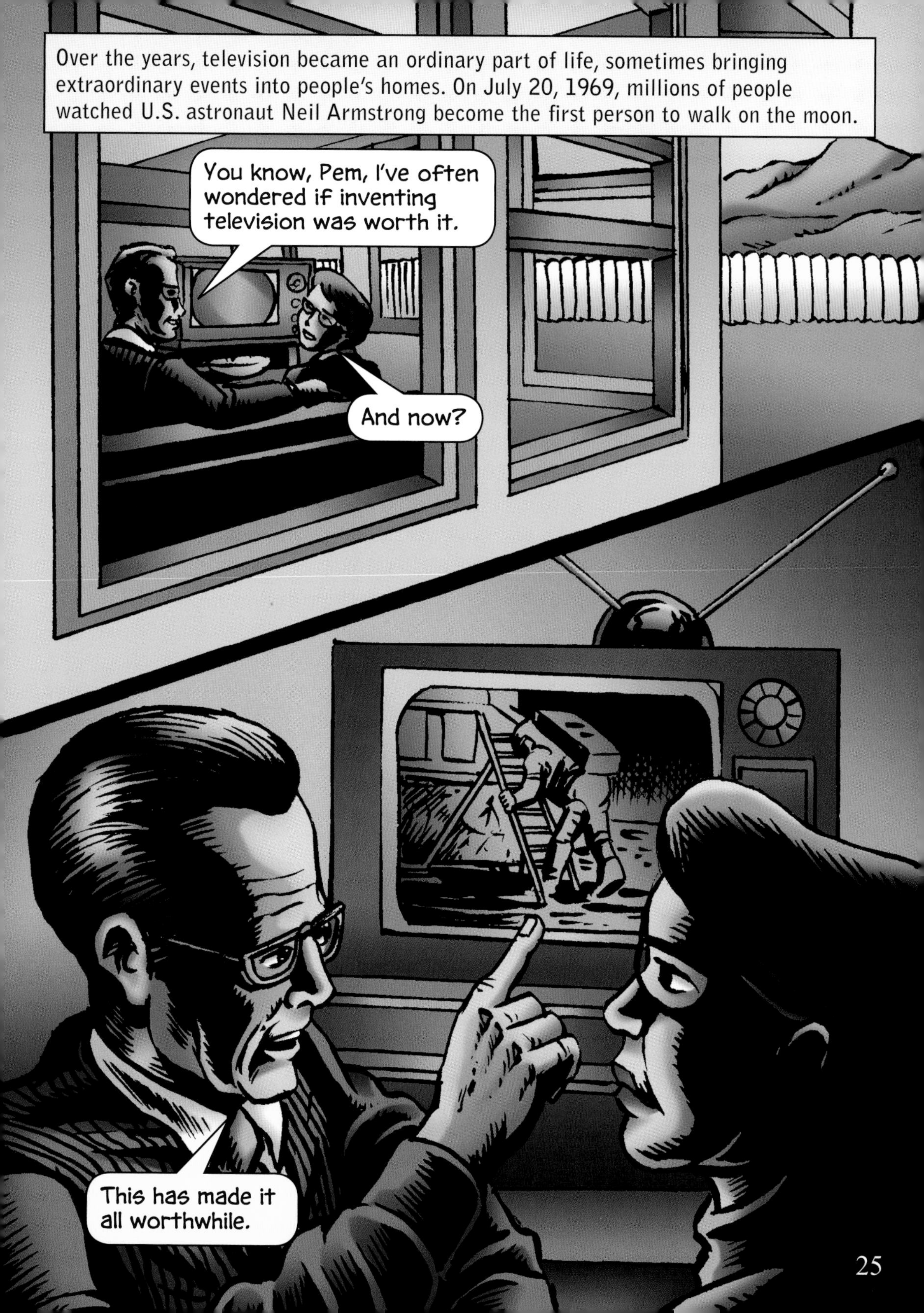
Over the years, television became an ordinary part of life, sometimes bringing extraordinary events into people's homes. On July 20, 1969, millions of people watched U.S. astronaut Neil Armstrong become the first person to walk on the moon.
You know, Pem, I've often wondered if inventing television was worth it.
And now?
This has made it all worthwhile.

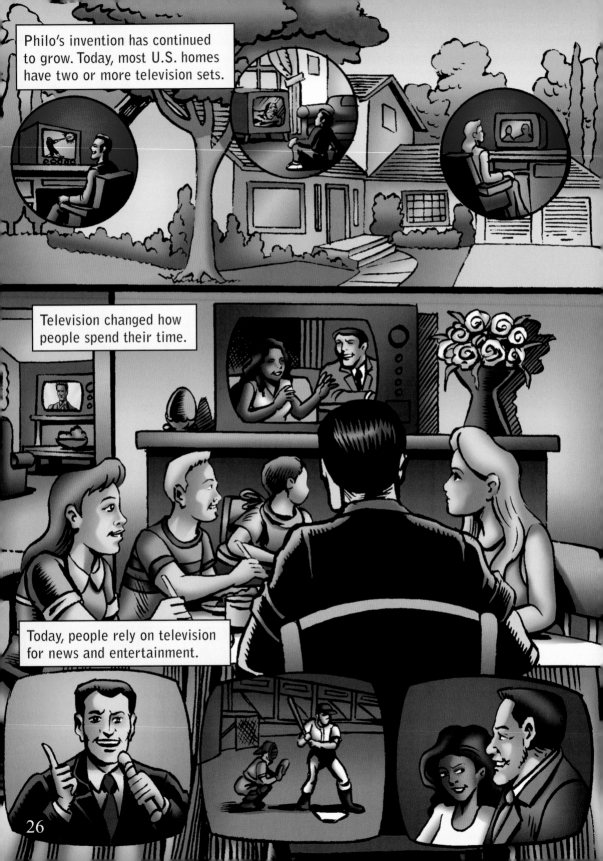

Philo's invention has continued to grow. Today, most U.S. homes have two or more television sets.

Television changed how people spend their time.

Today, people rely on television for news and entertainment.

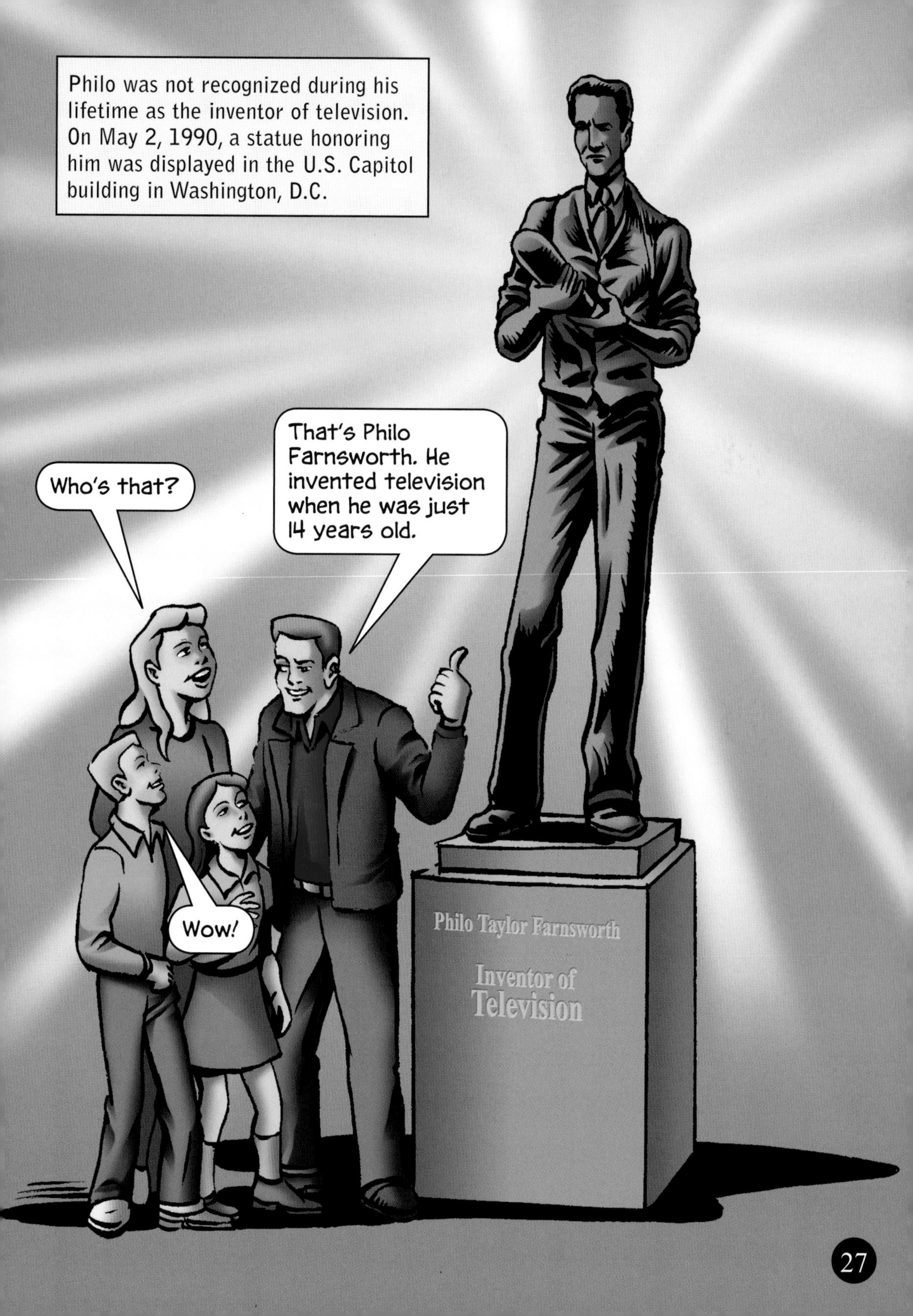
Philo was not recognized during his lifetime as the inventor of television. On May 2, 1990, a statue honoring him was displayed in the U.S. Capitol building in Washington, D.C.
Who's that?
That's Philo Farnsworth. He invented television when he was just 14 years old.
Wow!
Philo Taylor Farnsworth
Inventor of Television

MORE ABOUT FARNSWORTH AND THE TELEVISION

 Philo T. Farnsworth was born August 19, 1906, in Beaver City, Utah. He died March 11, 1971, at age 64.

 During World War II (1939–1945), Philo changed his Image Dissector into a sniperscope that made it possible for soldiers to see in the dark. He also developed a radar system that could spot and destroy an approaching missile for the military.

 In 1957, Philo was a guest on the television quiz show *I've Got a Secret*. No one on the panel could guess who he was. Host Gary Moore honored Philo by saying, "We'd all be out of work if it weren't for you."

 While Philo and his family lived in Fort Wayne, Indiana, they didn't have a television. When Philo's son Kent was in first grade, he discovered all his classmates had a television. Kent asked his dad to buy one for their family. Philo reluctantly agreed.

By 1967, almost every home had at least one television set. Today, most homes in the United States have at least two televisions. Most Americans watch more than four hours of television each day.

Philo received at least 150 U.S. patents for his inventions.

Time magazine named Philo one of the 100 most important people of the 20th century.

In 1994, Philo was named to the National Inventors Hall of Fame.

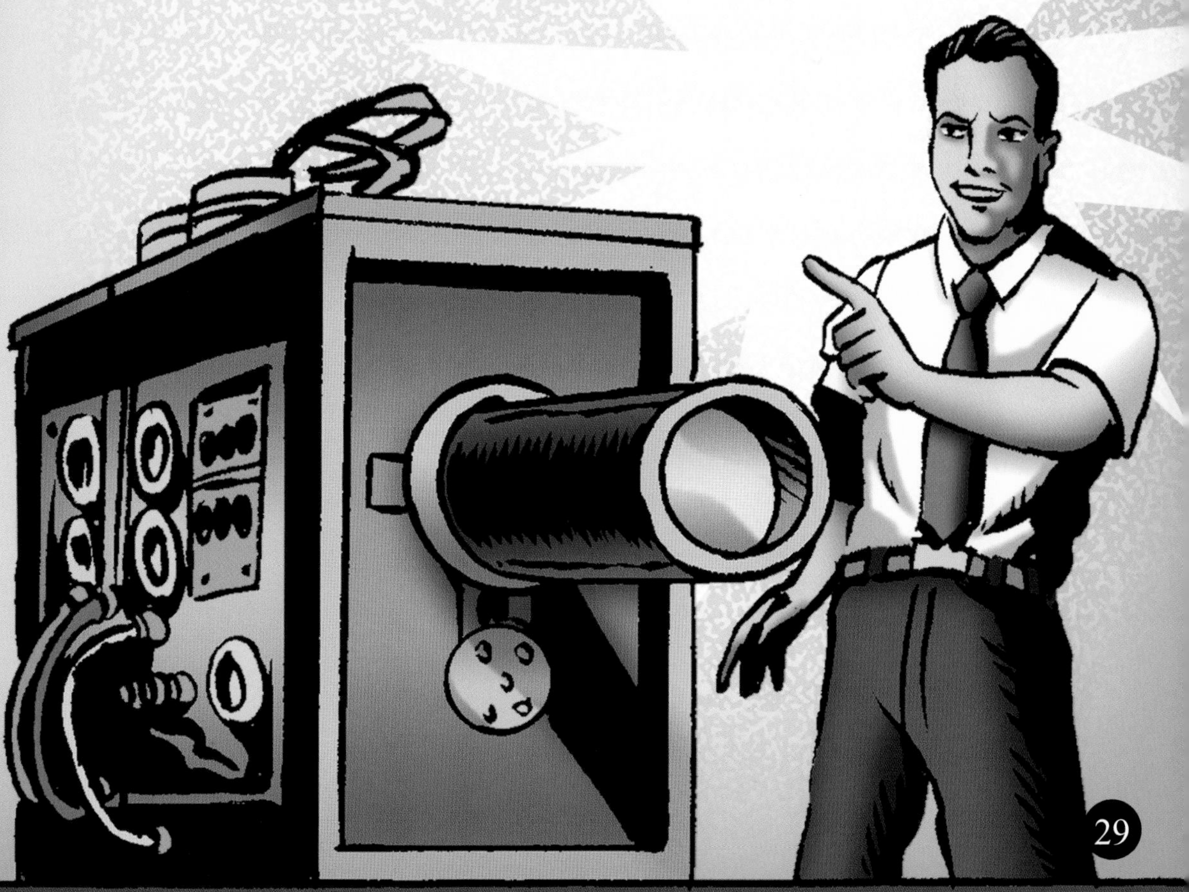

GLOSSARY

Image Dissector (IM-ij di-SEK-tur)—a machine that breaks images into electricity

Image Oscillite (IM-ij oss-UH-lyte)—a machine that receives an electronic signal and turns it into a television picture

invest (in-VEST)—to give or lend money to a company

license (LYE-suhnss)—a document that gives official permission to do something

network (NET-wurk)—a system of things that are connected to each other

patent (PAT-uhnt)—a legal document that gives an inventor the right to make, use, or sell an invention for a set number of years

INTERNET SITES

FactHound offers a safe, fun way to find Internet sites related to this book. All of the sites on FactHound have been researched by our staff.

Here's how:
1. Visit *www.facthound.com*
2. Choose your grade level.
3. Type in this book ID **0736864873** for age-appropriate sites. You may also browse subjects by clicking on letters, or by clicking on pictures and words.
4. Click on the **Fetch It** button.

FactHound will fetch the best sites for you!

READ MORE

Mattern, Joanne. *Television: Window to the World.* Reading Power. New York: PowerKids Press, 2003.

Nobleman, Marc Tyler. *The Television.* Great Inventions. Mankato, Minn.: Capstone Press, 2005.

Roberts, Russell. *Philo T. Farnsworth: The Life of Television's Forgotten Inventor.* Unlocking the Secrets of Science. Bear, Del.: Mitchell Lane, 2004.

Teitelbaum, Michael. *Radio and Television.* Great Inventions. Milwaukee: World Almanac Library, 2005.

BIBLIOGRAPHY

Everson, George. *The Story of Television; The Life of Philo T. Farnsworth.* New York: Arno Press, 1974.

Farnsworth, Elma G. *Distant Vision: Romance and Discovery on an Invisible Frontier.* Salt Lake City: PemberlyKent, 1990.

Schatzkin, Paul. *The Boy Who Invented Television: A Story of Inspiration, Persistence, and Quiet Passion.* Silver Spring, Md.: TeamCom Books, 2002.

INDEX

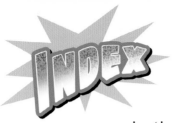